Archaeology and Ancient Cultures

UNCOVERING THE CULTURE OF

ANCIENT INDIA

By Alix Wood

PowerKiDS press.

NEW YORK

Published in 2016 by
The Rosen Publishing Group, Inc.
29 East 21st Street, New York, NY 10010

Cataloging-in-Publication Data

Wood, Alix.
Uncovering the culture of ancient India / by Alix Wood.
p. cm. — (Archaeology and ancient cultures)
Includes index.
ISBN 978-1-5081-4659-9 (pbk.)
ISBN 978-1-5081-4660-5 (6-pack)
ISBN 978-1-5081-4661-2 (library binding)
1. India — Civilization — To 1200 — Juvenile literature. 2. India — History — Juvenile literature.
3. India — Civilization — Juvenile literature. I. Wood, Alix. II. Title.
DS425.W66 2016
934—d23

Copyright © 2016 Alix Wood Books

Editor: Eloise Macgregor
Designer: Alix Wood
Consultant: Rupert Matthews

Photo Credits: Cover, 1, © Shutterstock; 2, 9 middle © DollarPhotoClub; 5 top © Aniketh M.J. and
Sulesh Kumar; 5 bottom © Nasli and Alice Heeramaneck Collection; 6 bottom, 13 bottom, 28 bottom,
29 © Bernard Gagnon; 7 top © Anubhab91; 7 bottom © Raveesh Vyas; 9 bottom © Soma Jha; 10 ©
epicycles; 11 bottom, 13 top, 17 bottom, 27 top © Trustees of the British Museum; 14 bottom right
© siddeshwar; 15 © Gwen Kelly; 16 top © Eames Collection, Chicago; 16 bottom © Ross Funnell; 17
top © Biswarup Ganguly; 18 © Los Angeles County Museum of Art; 19 © Giridharmamidi; 20 top
© Dr Ajay S. Sekher; 20-21 bottom © Augustus Binu; 21 top © Geological Survey of India; 22 © Jai
Bharat/The Maharaja Sansar Chand Museum; 23 © V.S. Sun; 24 top © Gowrishanker; 24-25 bottom
© S. Sriram; 25 top © Herbert Smith; 26 bottom © Saurav Sen Tonandada; 27 bottom © Vikramashila
Museum; 28 top © Kiranraj; all other images are in the public domain

Manufactured in the United States of America

CPSIA Compliance Information: Batch #: BW16PK For Further Information contact Rosen Publishing, New York, New York at 1-800-237-9932

CONTENTS

ANCIENT INDIA

Early man lived in caves in India more than 100,000 years ago. The earliest known civilization in India was along the valley of the River Indus. The people of the Indus Valley built very well-planned cities with luxuries such as water drains and public baths. They **manufactured** and **traded** goods with other countries. Their civilization and buildings were as advanced as that of the ancient Egyptians.

Until quite recently no one knew that the Indus Valley Civilization had existed. It was very exciting when **archaeologists** began to piece together what they had found, and form a picture of the people who lived there.

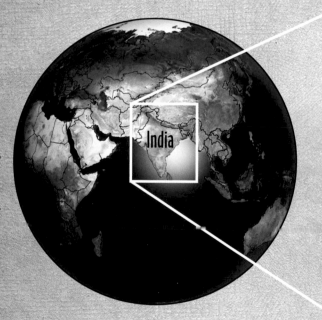

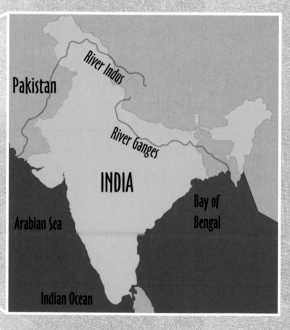

Timeline

A colored band by the page number shows each site's time period

c 5000 - 3000 BCE	c 3000 - 1700 BCE	c 1700 - 500 BCE	600 - 300 BCE
Neolithic	Indus Valley Civilization	Vedic Period	Mahajanapadas

The elephant stables at the old city of Hampi

Often, old buildings fall into disrepair. Alexander Cunningham, a British army engineer, was interested in the history and archaeology of India. In 1861, he founded the Archaeological Survey of India (ASI). Today, the ASI explore and preserve cultural monuments in India. A dig at Hampi, in 2015, has just unearthed some steps leading downward, which archaeologists believe may lead to a lost temple! New discoveries are being made all the time!

Artifact Facts

Buddhism is a religion that began in northeastern India. Alexander Cunningham was interested in the Buddhist religion. He liked to explore old Buddhist sites. This statue of Buddha was found when he dug at an old monastery at Nalanda.

230 BCE - 500 CE	700 - 1200 CE	1200 - 1700 CE
Classical India	Early Medieval Period	Late Medieval Period

BHIMBEKTA

Bhimbekta

Looking out of a train window one day, archaeologist V. S. Wakankar saw some rock **formations** that made him think. They looked just like formations he had seen in Spain and France which turned out to have caves with ancient paintings inside. He got off at the next stop and walked back to the area. The first cave he found had pictures on the wall!

Around 700 rock shelters have now been found in the region, 243 of them at Bhimbekta. The shelters were lived in more than 100,000 years ago by **Homo erectus**, an ancient **ancestor** of modern humans. Some of the paintings found in the Bhimbetka rock shelters are around 30,000 years old. The shelters also have what are believed to be the world's oldest stone walls and floors.

Indian archaeologist V. S. Wanaker

Paintings of people on horseback from a shelter at Bhimbekta.

The cave pictured right is the largest cave at Bhimbetka. The cave is not man-made, but has been made naturally. The rocks are quite smooth, so it appears the caves may have been made by water flowing through the rock, many thousands of years ago.

Human remains from around 10,000 years ago have been found in the caves. Gifts such as antlers and bone tools were found placed with the dead.

This large cave is believed to have been an assembly hall. People think the leader may have talked to the group while standing on the rock at the back of the hall.

THE INDUS VALLEY

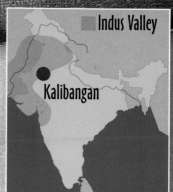

Indus Valley

Kalibangan

One of the earliest civilizations in the world made their home along the River Indus. The Indus Valley Civilization is partly in India and partly in Pakistan. The word "civilization" comes from the **Latin** word "civis," which means "city." The Indus Valley Civilization was made up of more than 1,400 towns and cities. The biggest cities were Harappa and Mohenjo-Daro which are now in Pakistan. In India, Kalibangan was a small, but important city.

The first people in the Indus Valley were hunters and **gatherers**, like other people around the world at this time. By around 4000 BCE the people began farming. They needed a good supply of water to grow crops, so by 2500 BCE many had settled by the River Indus.

Archaeologists at Kalibangan found some surprising things. The most important discovery was this plowed field! That may not sound very exciting, but it is one of the earliest plowed fields ever found. It proves that the people of Kalibangan were some of the earliest farmers.

Kalibangan's importance was discovered by an Italian, Luigi Pio Tessitori (left). He recognized that the ruins were extremely old and probably from an important, unknown culture. He wrote to a colleague about a **seal** he had found, saying it had "an inscription in characters which I am unable to identify. I suspect it is an extremely interesting find."

In 1919, Tessitori caught Spanish flu on a voyage back from Italy, and died. He never got a chance to show the seal to the Archaeological Survey of India (ASI). The knowledge of the seal was buried with him until businessman Hazarimal Banthia discovered copies of Tessitori's letters while visiting Italy!

An Indian postage stamp showing the seal found at Kalibangan.

Artifact Facts

Indus Valley people made toys. This bullock cart was made using baked clay. Archaeologists have found rattles, bird-whistles, model cows that waggle their heads, and monkeys that slide down rope! At Harappa archaeologists found dice that are probably the oldest in the world.

DHOLAVIRA

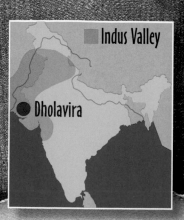

Indus Valley

Dholavira

Dholavira was an ancient city in the Indus Valley. It was built on an island in the middle of a large salt marsh, and believed to have been one of the grandest cities of its time. It had a **fortified** center with strong double walls for protection. Unusually, many of the buildings were made of stone rather than mud bricks. The site was discovered by archaeologist J. P. Joshi while working for the ASI. **Excavations** have shown that people lived at the site for over 1,500 years.

The people who built Dholavira had a clever way of saving water. Massive **reservoirs** were built from stone, and used to store water. Rainwater and water from two nearby streams were fed into the reservoirs using stone channels. In the desert several years may pass without rainfall, so systems like this were very important. The city also had a large well and a huge rectangular bathing tank, a little like a swimming pool.

Stone drainage channels at Dholavira

One of the city's wells

Indus Valley writing used picture-signs instead of an alphabet. No one yet has been able to understand the signs. Because the longest bit of writing found was only 26 characters long, experts find it very hard to find a clue to what the symbols mean. Some experts think their spoken language was similar to Tamil, which is spoken today by people in southern India and Sri Lanka.

Artifact Facts

One of the most important discoveries at Dholavira was this big wooden sign covered in symbols made from pieces of gypsum. When archaeologists found the sign it had fallen to the floor, and the wood had decayed. By patiently excavating the area, archaeologists made sure that the position of the letters on the floor survived.

This sign is one of the longest pieces of Indus writing ever found. One symbol appears four times. Can you beat the experts and try to figure out what it might say?

Many seals had symbols on them, like this one, found at Mohenjo-daro. Seals were probably used to close documents and mark packages. The seal was pressed into damp clay which was left to set. You could tell if a package had been opened if the seal was broken. Traders would presumably have been able to recognize what was written on the seals.

THE BEAD FACTORY

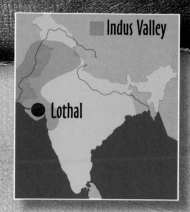

After Pakistan separated from India in 1947, the great Indus Valley sites of Harappa and Mohenjo-Daro went to Pakistan. The Indian government wanted to find some great sites of their own. Archaeologist S.R. Rao took up the challenge.

One day, while Rao was searching the countryside, his old jeep broke down. Rao had to stay overnight in a small village. The following morning he noticed a mound by the road. Rao kept pieces of broken pots decorated with **Harappan** painting in his pocket. He asked a local man passing on his bullock cart if he had seen any pieces like that at the mound. The man said yes, he had seen lots! The area had just had heavy monsoon rains, so Rao had to wade across fields of water to reach the mound. It was worth it, he found ancient clay pottery, beads, and a stone blade!

Rao had found the important Harappan site of Lothal. The site has now been excavated and archaeologists have discovered the remains of a dockyard, a warehouse, a **fortified** center, a drainage system, and several wells. Lothal has the world's earliest known dock.

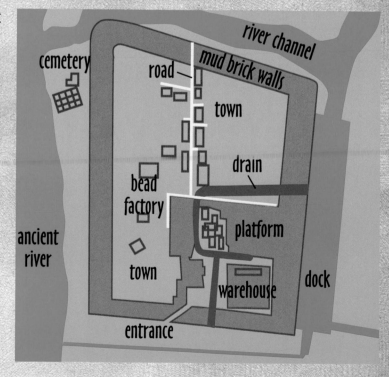

A map of the Lothal site

Beautiful etched carnelian beads from Lothal

Artifact Facts

Lothal's large bead factory had ten living rooms and a large workplace courtyard. The beads were traded by boat to countries as far away as West Asia and Africa.

Rao asked the village women to search for tiny beads during the dig. They were experts at it, as they were used to picking out tiny bits of dirt when they harvested wheat.

The museum at Lothal has a set of the tiny beads found at the site. They are so small that the museum supplies a magnifying glass, so that visitors can see them properly! Even in such tiny beads, each one has a hole to pass the thread through to make a necklace. The Indus Valley bead makers were incredibly skillful.

Houses in Lothal had bathrooms, believed to be the world's oldest bathrooms ever! People poured water on themselves while standing on the brick platform. The water would drain away.

drain

brick platform

BRAHMAGIRI

Brahmagiri

Very often when archaeologists dig at a site, they come across a confusing set of finds. The site may have been lived in over many hundreds or thousands of years, which makes it hard to date each object. The settlement at Brahmagiri was just such a place. When the head of the ASI at the time, Mortimer Wheeler, excavated Brahmagiri he found artifacts from many different time periods. Because of this, archaeologists dig carefully in layers. The finds near the surface tend to be newer than the deeper finds.

At Brahmagiri, Wheeler found ten Iron Age stone circles, built around 900 BCE. In the middle of the stone circles were stone-lined burial chambers called cists.

An excavated burial chamber

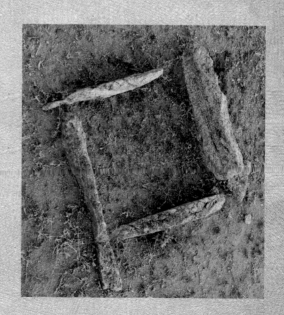

In this example only the central cist stones stick out of the ground.

After the Iron Age, the Indian ruler Emperor Ashoka, of the powerful Mauryan Empire, ruled the region. Ashoka was a ruthless ruler, until he became a Buddhist. Buddhism is a religion that encourages peace and Ashoka turned to it after regretting a very bloody war that he had fought.

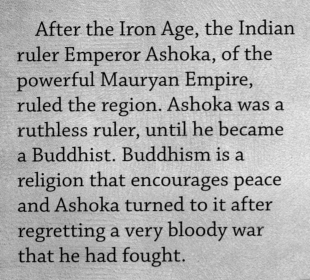

Artifact Facts

This carved stone found at Brahmagiri is one of several Ashokan rock **edicts**. They date from between 269 - 232 BCE, when Emperor Ashoka ruled the area. The writing describes the Emperor's attempts at solving society's problems. Ashoka wanted them to be read by the local people and translated them into the local language.

A stone circle made from boulders at Brahmagiri

AHICHATRA

Ahichatra

The Indus Valley Civilization gradually disappeared. No one is too sure why, but it may have been a mixture of war, disease, and hunger. In around 1500 BCE, groups of people from the area between the Black Sea and the Caspian Sea moved into the Indus Valley area. These people were known as Aryans. They brought their own religious traditions with them. An area east of the Indus Valley, known as Panchala, was divided into two kingdoms, with the River Ganges between them.

Ahichatra was the capital of the northern kingdom, during this time, known as the Vedic Period. The time period got its name because it was when the Vedas, the oldest **scriptures** of Hinduism, were written. They were written in the language Vedic Sanskrit.

Above is a copy of the Rigveda. There are four Vedas; the Rigveda, Yajurveda, Samaveda, and Atharvaveda.

The River Ganges

At Ahichatra, archaeologists have found many examples of painted gray ware bowls and dishes, like the piece below. An ancient Indian culture from around the middle and late Vedic period is known as the Painted Gray Ware culture, because of the amount of similar pots found from the period. The first ever finds were excavated at Ahichatra.

Painted gray ware is a fine, gray pottery painted with geometric patterns in black.

A typical piece of painted gray ware, from between 1000-600 BCE. This bowl must have been baked in an enclosed oven as it was very evenly baked.

Artifact Facts

Some of the ancient art found decorating the temple at Ahichatra is very beautiful. This plaque comes on a monument dedicated to the Hindu god, Shiva. It may show a fight between Shiva, disguised as a hunter, and Arjuna, from a well-known story.

KAMPILYA

Kampilya

While Ahichatra was the capital north of the River Ganges, Kampilya was the capital of the southern kingdom of Panchala. It was a very important city, and had been capital of the whole of Panchala before the country was divided.

The city of Kampilya is mentioned in the **epic** poem the *Mahabharata*. The *Mahabharata* is one of two major Sanskrit epics of ancient India, the other being the *Ramayana*. The heroes of the story are the five Pandava brothers. They fight their evil cousins, the Kaurava brothers, to see who will rule the region. With the help of many Hindu gods, especially Krishna, the Pandavas win.

Archaeologists searching for the city of Kampilya are now sure it is near the modern day village of Kampil.

This illustration from the *Mahabharata* shows the Pandava brothers at the court of King Drupad, whose palace was at Kampilya.

The ruins of a mound and ancient temple near Kampil.

The architects who built Kampilya were very precise in their design. The walls surrounding the city are perfectly in line with the points of the compass. What is very surprising about this layout is that another much older city, Dholavira (page 10-11), has precisely the same feature! Dholavira is 2,000 years older than Kampilya. Archaeologists believe that this proves that knowledge, customs, and beliefs from the Indus Valley Civilization were passed down over thousands of years to these more recent civilizations.

Artifact Facts

These small pillars found at a temple in Kampilya are known as Shiv lings. They are thought to represent the energy of the Hindu god, Shiva. The temple is believed to have been founded by the wise man, Agastya, who features in the epic poem, the Ramayana.

A BUSY PORT

Pattanam

Pattanam was an Indian port with a long history. The earliest finds are from 1,000 BCE. The port traded with Rome between 100 BCE and 400 CE. Some experts believe that Pattanam is part of a famous lost port called Muziris, which is described in many ancient Tamil and Roman texts.

Archaeologists dated the site by studying charcoal and wood samples taken from the Iron Age layer. Exciting finds at the site include square copper coins from the beginning of the Christian era. Archaeologists found Roman pots for transporting goods, and other much finer Roman and Chinese pottery. They found evidence of jewelry-making, digging up hundreds of glass beads and bead-making molds. They even found a wharf structure, along with a 2,000-year-old, 19.7-foot (6 m) wooden dugout canoe!

Layers of history at Pattanam

"Pattanam" means "port city," but Pattanam is surrounded by land. The Periyar River, pictured, once flowed much closer to the site than it does today.

Artifact Facts

When archaeologists dig, they have to work from the top down. However, the city would have been created from the bottom up. It is very important to preserve or record artifacts they discover as they dig through the layers. This Pattanam brick structure's shape is preserved, but archaeologists dig all around it looking for deeper, earlier finds.

The amount of artifacts and structures found at Pattanam means they must have had a large, skilled workforce in the city. Blacksmiths made iron objects such as nails and tools. Coppersmiths made coins, and goldsmiths made ornaments. Potters made a huge quantity of pots, lamps, ovens, and other objects. Brick makers, bricklayers, and roofers must have used the large amount of bricks and roof-tiles found. Bead makers, stonecutters, and polishers worked in the jewelry trade. Weavers also worked at the site, as their tools have been found. Pattanam must have been a busy, important port.

KANGRA FORT

Kangra

The fort at Kangra is perched on top of a steep cliff overlooking the Manjhi and Banganga Rivers. It is believed to be the oldest fort in India. The fort we see today was occupied during the Katoch dynasty around 1500 BCE. Archaeologists believe there may have been a fort on the site before that. The Katoch dynasty is believed to be the oldest royal dynasty in the world, starting at around 4300 BCE. They are mentioned in the Hindu epics *Ramayana* and *Mahabharata*.

The fort has been attacked many times. Kangra Fort was never destroyed during the many battles it saw, however, but by a massive earthquake in 1905.

Kangra Fort before the 1905 earthquake

The fort after the earthquake

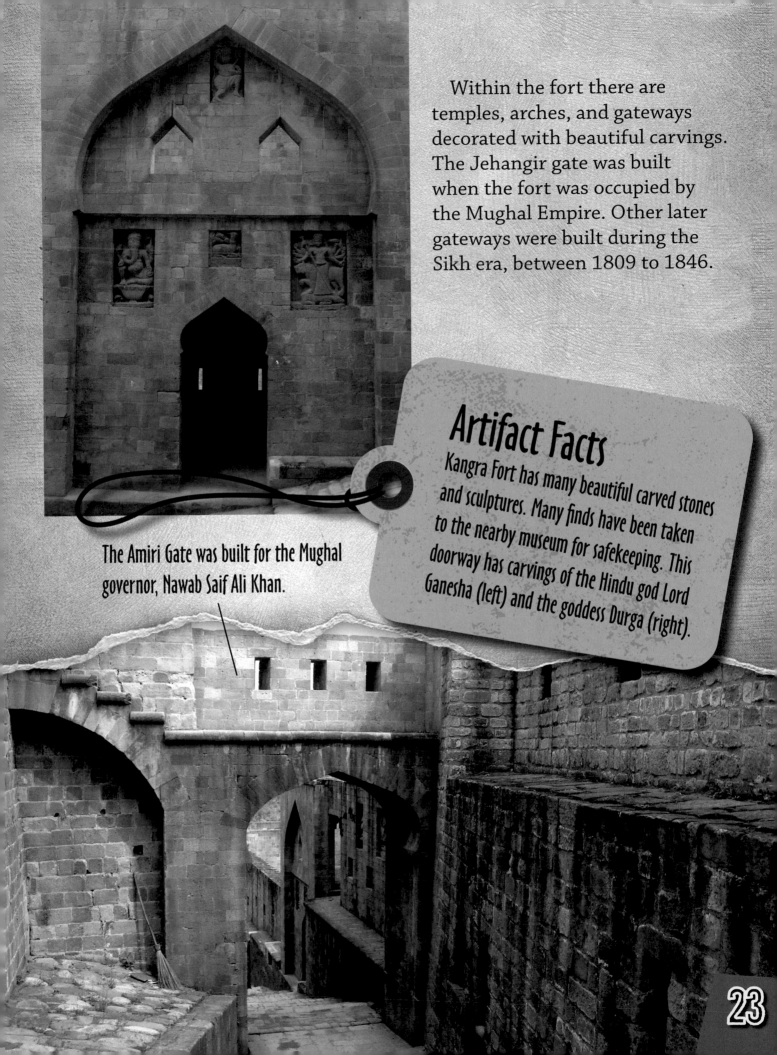

Within the fort there are temples, arches, and gateways decorated with beautiful carvings. The Jehangir gate was built when the fort was occupied by the Mughal Empire. Other later gateways were built during the Sikh era, between 1809 to 1846.

The Amiri Gate was built for the Mughal governor, Nawab Saif Ali Khan.

Artifact Facts

Kangra Fort has many beautiful carved stones and sculptures. Many finds have been taken to the nearby museum for safekeeping. This doorway has carvings of the Hindu god Lord Ganesha (left) and the goddess Durga (right).

MAHABALIPURAM

Mahabalipuram

Mahabalipuram was an ancient seaport. Chinese and Roman coins from around 300 CE have been found at the site. In the 800s the king, Narasimhavarman, built wonderful temples carved out of rock along the coast. Sailors called the port "Seven Pagodas" after the seven temples that stood on the shore. Now, only the Shore Temple (left) survives.

the Shore Temple

Five smaller monuments, known as the Pancha Rathas, were carved out of vast granite boulders. They are named after five brothers from the epic poem the *Mahabharata*; Dharmaraja, Bhima, Arjuna, Nakula, Sahadeva, and their wife, Draupadi. The sculptors were so skilled that some think Mahabalipuram may have been home to a sculpture school.

Draupadi Ratha

Arjuna Ratha

Nakula Sahadeva Ratha

What happened to the other six temples of Mahabalipuram? No one was too sure. Local legend said the gods were jealous of Mahabalipuram's beauty, and sent a flood to bury it beneath the waves.

A **tsunami** hit the coast of India in 2004. A tsunami is caused by an earthquake under the ocean, which pulls the water away from the land for a period before giant waves surge back toward the land. While the water pulled away, local people saw buildings uncovered near the shore!

Since then, divers have explored the area of sea near Mahabalipuram and discovered many underwater buildings.

Artifact Facts
The 2004 tsunami made some lasting changes to the coastline. Areas that had been under the ocean were now beach. Statues like these, from the lost temples, can now be seen on the shore!

Bhima Ratha

Dharmaraja Ratha

A GREAT UNIVERSITY

Vikramashila University was one of the most important centers of learning. It was established by King Dharmapala after the teaching standard was believed to have become poor at another great university at Nalanda. Vikramashila was destroyed during fighting in around 1200 CE. The remains of the ancient university were excavated by Indian archaeologist B. P. Sinha of Patna University, and later by the Archaeological Survey of India.

The digs unearthed a huge monastery with a cross-shaped **stupa** in its center. A stupa is a Buddhist place of worship. The monastery where the monks lived formed a large open square around the stupa. There were 208 bedrooms. Some of the rooms had arched chambers beneath them, possibly where monks could **meditate** in private.

Vikramashila

— the main stupa

a seating and meditation area

The stupa had four chambers to the north, south, east, and west. Each chamber had an enormous image of a seated Buddha. Terraced walkways were decorated with moldings and terracotta plaques showing gods and Buddhist scenes as well as scenes of daily life and animal figures.

Artifact Facts

Pictured is one of the large Buddha statues found at the Vikramashila stupa. The smaller sculptures around the Buddha represent major events in Buddha's life.

Archaeologists discovered some amazing buildings at Vikramashila. The library building was air conditioned by cooled water from a reservoir which ran through vents in the back wall! The system was probably meant to help preserve the old, delicate books.

The design of the central stupa and terracotta plaques are like those at another monastery, Somapura Mahavihar, in Bangladesh, also founded by King Dharmapala. Perhaps he used the same architects?

One of the terracotta plaques from Vikramashila

KONARK SUN TEMPLE

Konark

onark Sun Temple is believed to have been built around 1250 CE for King Narasimhadeva. The temple is in the shape of a gigantic chariot. The sun god, Surya, is believed to sit in a chariot as he moves across the sky. The temple is pulled by seven carved horses and has 24 enormous stone wheels carved on its sides!

lion

elephant

man

Konark fell into ruin. Experts who analyzed moss-covered rocks believe the temple was abandoned around 1573. The marshy land may have caused the buildings to collapse, or lightning or an earthquake may have caused damage. Some believe the temple was never properly completed. Gradually many of the stones and sculptures were removed and used for other buildings.

The entrance is guarded by two huge lions, each killing a war elephant who is crushing a man. It is believed that lions represent pride, elephants represent wealth, and both of them harm man.

At one time a much taller main tower stood behind this meeting hall.

According to local legend, the temple had two very powerful magnets built into the tower that allowed Surya's throne to hover in midair! After many shipwrecks along the coast the magnets were removed as they disrupted ship's compasses. The main temple tower finally collapsed in 1848. Perhaps the magnets had held it together? To preserve the meeting hall, it was filled with stones and sand. Trees were planted between the temple and the sea to stop sand blowing in and wearing away the carvings.

Artifact Facts

Imagine finding a crocodile like this one, hidden in the sand. In 1909, the Mayadevi temple at Konark was discovered while workers were removing sand and debris around the site!

GLOSSARY

ancestor One from whom an individual, group, or species is descended.

archaeologists Scientists that study past human life, fossils, monuments and tools left by ancient peoples.

Buddhism A religion of eastern and central Asia growing out of the teaching of Gautama Buddha.

edicts A law or order made or given by an authority, such as a ruler.

epic A long poem telling of the deeds of a hero and often centering on the ideals of a nation or culture.

excavations The area uncovered by digging away covering earth.

formations A bed of rocks or series of beds recognizable as a unit.

fortified Strengthened by military defenses.

gatherers People who harvest wild food.

Harappan From a Bronze Age culture that flourished in the Indus valley.

Homo erectus An extinct species of early man.

Latin The language spoken in ancient Rome.

manufactured Made from raw materials by hand or by machinery.

meditate To spend time in quiet thinking.

reservoirs An artificial or natural lake where water is collected as a water supply.

scriptures The sacred writings of a religion.

seal A usually ornamental adhesive stamp that may be used to close a letter or package.

stupa A dome-shaped building built as a Buddhist shrine.

traded Exchanged, purchased, or sold goods to another.

tsunami A great sea wave produced especially by an earthquake or volcano eruption under the sea.

FURTHER INFORMATION

Books

Ali, Daud. *Hands-On History! Ancient India: Discover the Rich Heritage of the Indus Valley and the Mughal Empire.* London, UK: Armadillo, 2014.

Dalal, Anita. *National Geographic Investigates: Ancient India: Archaeology Unlocks the Secrets of India's Past.* Des Moines, IA: National Geographic Children's Books, 2007.

Williams, Brian. *Daily Life in the Indus Valley Civilization* (Daily Life in Ancient Civilizations). Portsmouth, NH: Heinemann, 2015.

Due to the changing nature of Internet links, PowerKids Press has developed an online list of websites related to the subject of this book. This site is updated regularly. Please use this link to access the list:

www.powerkidslinks.com/AAC/India

INDEX